500 Tips for Marketing Your Crafts

by A. B. Petrow

Published by CraftMasters™ Books
Sebastopol, California

ISBN-10: 0-9655193-6-8
ISBN-13: 978-0-9655193-6-6

Cover painting by Rhonda Libby

Printed in USA by PrintingSystem.com

Introduction

This is a collection of tips for artists and craftspeople to help you sell what you make. You might start by marketing your craft creations at craft fairs. The first section consists of tips about how to find craft fairs, how to get into them, and how to survive them and make money.

To even out your income, tips for wholesale marketing of your crafts to craft galleries is covered in the second section.

The third area covered is selling through the Internet, where you can either make your own web site or put your crafts on a web catalog or eBay.

Finally, there are tips about general business, pricing, planning, bookkeeping, etc.

I have been making and selling my crafts (jewelry and woodwork) for over 30 years at craft fairs and art shows in 29 states. I have made a good living from it, and have had an interesting crafts career, with lots of free time and travel.

I want to help new artists and craftspeople make a living selling their crafts by sharing some of the information I have learned. These tips would have been invaluable to me when I started out. My hope here is that from these 500 tips, you will glean at least a few that might save you hundreds of hours, or hundreds of dollars, and make this book purchase very worthwhile.

Table of Contents

13

Craft Fairs

The first section of this list of tips is about craft fairs. A weekend craft fair or art show is a good place to start your business. Selling directly to the user of your product will help you find out what the public wants. Even if you eventually want to market your products mostly by selling wholesale to craft galleries, you can test your product by doing occasional craft fairs. You also can make a very good living doing only craft fairs.

Finding the show

1.   Subscribe to a craft fair guide for your area.

You will need a magazine with a list of shows. Then you write the show's promoter for more information and an application. There is a list of craft fair guides at www.craftshowplace.com.

2.   Go to a show and talk to the craftspeople.

Ask local artists how they find out about shows. They will probably tell you about a craft fair guide.

3.   Do a Google search to find shows.

Search for craft shows in your area. For example, type "craft fair california" and hit search. You will instantly get lots of suggestions.

4.   Calculate the potential of the show.

Multiply the attendance number by $10 (half of the people will spend $20 and half will spend nothing) and divide it by the number of artists. 50,000 people equals $1,000,000 divided by 250 artists equals an average of $4,000 per artist.

5. Use www.festivalnet.com.

The membership fee is about $50 a year. Search the site by state and month, and you will get all the shows in the state. One way to tell if it is a good show is by the booth fee. If it is under $100, it is probably too small of a show to make much money . A rule of thumb is that you should make 10x the show fee for it to be a good show.

6. Check out Art Fair Sourcebook.

This book is very helpful if you want to travel to bigger shows in other states.. It gives you tons of information about each of the top 300 shows in the country. A subscription for one year is about $200.00. www.artfairsourcebook.com 800-358-2045

Getting into the show

7. Read the craft fair application thoroughly.

Every craft fair has different requirements. Some require a workshop photo, a copy of your driver's license, or a resume.

8. Apply to the show early.

Early applications are often juried first. Jurors become bleary eyed after a while. They might look at 5,000 slides in a few days. You want them to be impressed with your slides early in the process.

17

9. Organize your fair applications.

Label twelve folders with the months of the year. When you get an application, write down the deadline on a deadline list, and write the show date on a calendar. Then put the application in the folder for the month of the show.

10. Your work should be consistent.

Jurors are looking for attention to detail, artistic mastery of materials, structure, and concept.

11. You have to grab their attention.

They look for whimsy, originality, and how everything works together. They are also comparing your work to all the other work juried.

12. Watch out for extended deadlines.

Sometimes an extended deadline means the show has a shortage of applicants, which indicates it might not be a very good show.

13.   Make your descriptions precise.

If the show asks for a 25-word description, do not give more or less. Your description will probably be read to the jury. If it is too long, it won't be read in full, and if it is short, you are missing an opportunity to tell the jurors what they can't see in your slides, such as process, texture, materials, use, etc.

Photography

14.   Jurors look at slides for 5 to 15 seconds.

Use slides of your most colorful work, so jurors will notice them.

15.   Make your slides with a 35mm or digital camera.

It doesn't have to be fancy. It should have manual settings so you can control your depth of field.

16.   Use a 50mm lens with a macro feature.

You can get one of these on eBay for less than $100. The macro feature will help you fill the image with your product if you make small items such as jewelry.

17.   Get a set of close-up lenses for small objects.

A set of close-up lenses includes a #1, #2, and #3. Use a step-up ring, and larger close-up lenses, to prevent softness around the edges. The center of a close-up lens is sharper than the edge. For example, use 58mm filters on a 52mm lens, with an adapter.

18.   Use a neutral background, nothing fancy.

Don't use plaids, weavings, etc. Uncluttered is the key. Indoors use white paper, outdoors use white roll paper or a white sheet.

19.   Use 500 watt bulbs for indoor shots.

Use Ektachrome 64 indoors with white photofloods.

20.   Use Fuji Provia or Velvia, ISO 100, slide film.

Outdoors, Velvia will give you saturated bright colors, while Provia gives you more natural colors. You can use this film indoors if you have blue photofloods. If you don't have blue photofloods, use a blue 80A filter on your camera lens.

21.   Turn off all flourescent lights.

If there is a fluorescent light on anywhere in the room, it will add an unwelcome green tint to your photo.

22.   Shoot in outdoor shade for even lighting.

Use the shady side of the house. The shady side is usually on the north side.

23.   Use f16 or f22 for depth of field.

Depth of field is the area of the image that is in focus, from front to back. If your camera has an "A" setting (aperture priority setting), set your f-stop at f22 and the camera will set the shutter speed. Everything will be in focus.

24.   Use f4 to blur background.

You might want to focus on one special detail of your work, or just remove an ugly background.

25.   Use a graduated background.

You can get it at from Superior Specialties, 800-666-2545 www.superspec.com I like the #9, black to white, and the #37, blue to white.

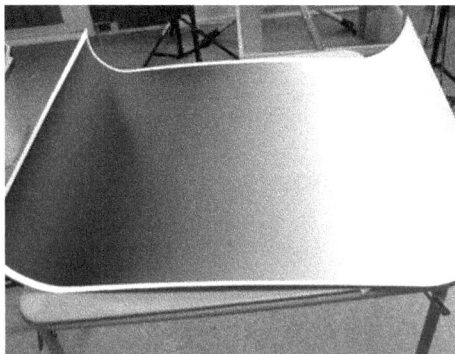

26.   Be sure your lens is clean.

Use only a commercial lens cleaning cloth on your lens. Anything else can scratch the coating on the lens.

27.   Always use a tripod.

Depth of field requires a slower shutter speed, and the longer shutter opening time increases the chance of camera shake.

28.   Use either a cable release or the camera timer.

You won't shake the camera and get a fuzzy picture.

29.   Write down settings for every shot you take.

When you get the slides back, you can match the best shots with the settings, for future reference. You won't have to relearn the entire process every time you make slides.

30.   Photograph only one item per slide.

Jurors need to focus on your product.

31.   Fill the frame.

You don't want the item to look small on the screen. At least one slide of wearables and jewelry could show a piece being worn, so the jurors know what it is.

32.   Use an 8x loupe and a light box.

Look at your slides closely to see if they are sharp or not. Slides should be clear and in sharp focus. You can get a cheap light box at a camera store for about $30.

33.   Project your slides.

Get a cheap slide projector to see your slides in full size as a jury will.

34.   Look at your slides as a group.

Put them together. They should have a consistency of vision. Check out the color relationships. Look for a theme.

35.   Projection shortens the life of a slide.

Every couple of years you will need new slides, even if you don't have a new product. Keep a set of master slides and make duplicates when necessary.

36.   Override the camera's light meter.

The built-in light meter in the camera will overexpose dark items, and underexpose light items.

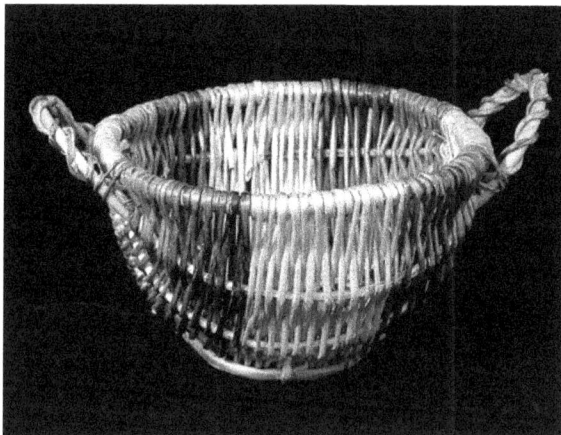

37.   Use a light tent for small items.

I use an EZ cube Light Tent. They are available on eBay for $45 to $90, depending on the size. Use three photofloods, two on the sides and one on the top.

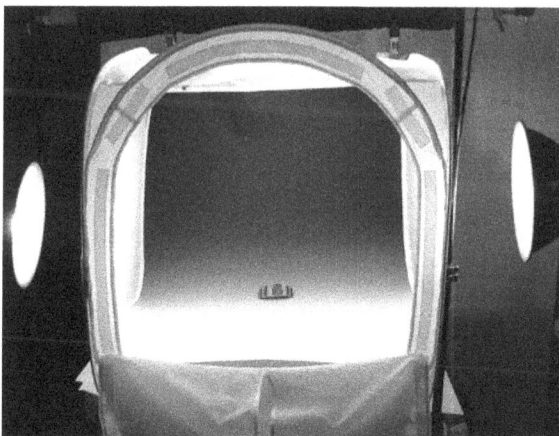

38.   Make your own light cube.

You can make a light cube out of translucent panels from Home Depot. They are in the flourescent fixture department. They come in 2' by 4'. You can cut them down to 2' by 2', and tape the edges together to make a cube with one side open. You can also make a cube out of 24" pieces of pvc covered with white cloth.

39.   Photograph 2D art against a black background.

Black velvet works well.

40.   Store your slides upright.

They should not rub against each other.

41.   Use a Kodak Picture Maker for quick prints.

There are 40,000 print making machines in the US. They are at most photograph shops, Costco, etc. They will make prints from a slide, negative, or a computer image on your CD.

42.   Don't let photographer keep your copyright.

Do not use a photographer who keeps the copyright to your photos. If you do, then you have to get slide duplicates from them.

43.   Put a copyright notice on your slides.

Avery #8167 labels will fit on a slide. It should say "Artwork © 2004 (Your Name)." Some shows don't allow labels because they cause jams. Use a Sharpie ULTRA fine Point marker.

44.   Have 5 slides duplicated at a time.

When having slides copied by a lab, have at least 5 made of the same image at a time to reduce wear on the originals. Always specify 1:1 when getting slides made, so that nothing gets cropped.

45.   Consider a digital camera.

You can use a digital camera to take your photos. Most of the information above applies to digital cameras. You can adjust your photos in Elements or Photoshop, and email the file to slides.com. They will make slides from your digital files for around $2.50 each.

Booth shots

46.   Use a wide-angle lens for booth photos.

A 28mm to 35mm lens will work best. Stand on a stool for a better angle, if necessary.

47.   Shoot your booth shot from a slight angle.

Remove all clutter. Make the work stand out. Compare your booth shot to your product photos. They should be the same quality. No people in the photo.

48.   Overexpose outdoor booth shots.

If you don't, the booth will look dark because the meter in the camera will expose for the sky. A cloudy day will provide even light.

49.   Use flash on indoor booth shots.

Try to get light into the corners of the booth.

Display

50.   Display your work in a "real life environment."

Your customer will be able to picture it in a real life situation. Towels in a towel rack, bottle stoppers in a bottle, barrettes on a wig, etc.

51.   Brighten up your booth.

A well-lit festive booth will attract more customers than a dark, dingy booth.

52.   Display photos of your technique.

Put them on the wall in your booth. Laminate and display any magazine articles about your products, and put them on the wall, too.

53.   Get the heaviest E-Z UP.

A heavier canopy is better in bad weather. 800-625-3607. Comes to over 100 lbs with the heavy walls.

54. You can use an E-Z UP indoors.

Remove the top and cover the corner poles with cloth. Also cover the top pieces with fireproof cloth. You will have lots of tubes to hang your lights from, and it won't tip over.

55.   Use a Trimline Canopy in really bad weather.

This is a different look than the E-Z UP, and takes about 20 minutes longer to set up. Florida artists use them. Flourish Company, 800-296-0049. Flourish also sells mesh panels for 2D art.

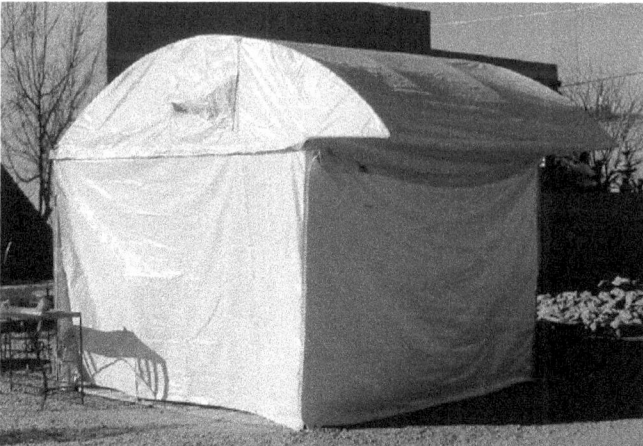

56.   Use a Craft Hut for hurricane areas.

They have steel legs and will not leak. Don't forget to use the cross-brace. Also from Flourish (see above).

57.   Always use the top cross brace on a Craft Hut.

If you don't, the arches can blow in toward the middle, and the top will fill with water during rainstorms and collapse the entire tent.

58.   Get zippers on both front and back.

Awnings are attached to a Craft Hut with zippers. When you order walls, you can get them with three panels in front, two in back. You can open one panel in the rain to let customers in. You can raise one of the panels in the back for shade.

59.   Use a Light Dome in windy areas.

This canopy does not blow over when properly weighted. It doesn't even move in the wind. Creative Energies, 800-851-8889

60.   You can also use a Light Dome indoors.

The large round cross-poles hold curtains well.

61.   Use Propanels for fine art and wall hangings.

www.propanels.com 214-350-5765

62.   Use lightweight mesh panels for 2D art.

You can cover them with cloth. Use curtain hooks that poke through the cloth into the mesh.

63.   Check out Gridlock Display System.

They offer 3x3 segments for displaying 2D art, and are easier to carry in small spaces. 48-D Cabot St, West Babylon, NY 11704 516-752-7502

64.   Don't use swing-arm lights.

They never look right. Also don't use the clamp-on lights with big aluminum reflectors. Use track lights from Home Depot.

65.   Be on the lookout for better display ideas.

Check out the other booths at a show. You can learn a lot from watching your neighbors set up and take down their booths.

66.   Use drop down bamboo rollups for walls.

8-foot rollups attached to your EZ-up frame with shower curtain hooks will make your booth seem cozier. They allow air circulation on a hot day, while providing some privacy from the booth next to you. You never know who you are going to be next to. The only drawback is that 8 feet is too long for a car. 2 four-foot rollups can be used instead.

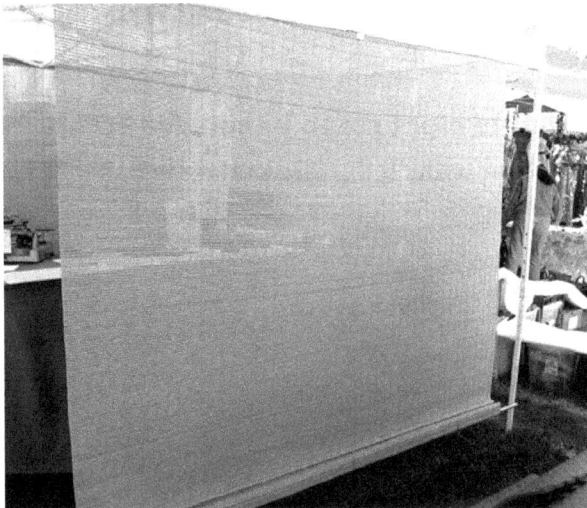

67.   Use pedestals for some shows.

The Howard Allen shows in Florida recommend that everything be displayed on a pedestal. Pedestals are available from Armstrong Products in Oklahoma-800-278-4279 www.armstrongproducts.com

68.   Put price stickers on every product you sell.

You don't want the customer to think you are making up the price. You won't waste time with a customer who couldn't afford the item.

69.   Use colored dot stickers.

Some crafters put colored dot stickers on the product, and then post a code to help the customer translate the prices. This allows you to change all prices up or down quickly by changing the code sign.

70.   Put big photos of your crafts on the wall.

Big photos behind or around the booth will help sell small items. They can also show your product being used. You can get a slide or print blown up to a 20" x 30" poster on foam-core at Kinko's for under $75. Kodak, through photo stores, offers unmounted 20 x 30 posters from your slides for $29.95.

71.   Have the photos laminated.

If your photos are laminated on both sides, they will hang easier and won't be damaged by water. For indoor shows, mount them on foam core from an art supply store

72.   Use grommets to hang up your photos.

They will keep the photos from ripping. Tie them up with thin strong wire.

73.   Frame your photos for indoor shows.

Use non-glare Plexiglas instead of glass.

74.   Use a banner for very large outdoor shows.

A banner will be seen over the heads of the sea of people. A return customer can find you from across the street. Get banners from Kinko's, 2 1/2' by 9', with grommets on the corners.

75.   Suspend your banner between two 10' poles.

Attach the poles to your canopy legs with clamps. Use steel conduit from Home Depot. Hook the grommeted banner to the poles with bungee cords. Use a couple of clamps to keep the banner from sliding down the poles.

76.   Display your booth number.

Put your booth number on the front of your booth. Your space number prominently displayed will help people find your booth again, especially if you are in a river of people, or off the beaten path. It will help the judges find you if you win an award.

77.   Use a booth sign indoors.

It should not look like your outdoor banner. It should reflect your style, but should not be plastic or garish. If the name of your city is on it, customers will start conversations about where you are from.

78.   Use black curtains indoors.

The background should not be noticeable. If not black, neutral colors are best.

79.   Use white walls outdoors.

White will reflect the light into your booth and brighten up your crafts in the shade.

80.   Hang a curtain over a corner of your booth.

Use the space for a changing room or storage.

81.   Make a portfolio or scrapbook.

Take slides and prints, put them in a scrapbook along with pics of your lifestyle. Customers can browse this while waiting.

82.   Display items at various heights.

This increases the visual appeal of your booth. Small items in your booth should be closer to eye level. Makes your crafts easy to reach.

83.   Make your table taller.

Use PVC tubing to make leg extensions to make your table taller.

84.   Clean your entire display every three shows.

You should wash the canopy and walls from top to bottom. Be sure they are thoroughly dry before storing, to avoid mildew.

Before the show

85.   Read and reread all the show information.

Learn the set-up times, days, etc. Know the show hours. Reread the show information a week before the show.

86.   Make an artist's statement for your booth.

Your artist's statement will tell what inspires you, what techniques you use, what is unique about your process. Frame it and hang it on the wall of your booth or in a plastic stand on a table top.

87.   Take three times as much stock to the show.

If you have three times as much stock as you expect to sell, and you sell twice as much as you expected, you will still have a well-stocked booth for the last customers at the show.

88.   Make a check list of show necessities.

Check your list just before you leave home.

My list of show necessities:
Gift boxes
Card inserts
Bags
VISA machine, thermal paper, and charger
VISA signage
Calculator
Sample of work in progress
Banner
Stakes
Ropes
Booth sign
Statement of purpose (artist's statement)
Price stickers
Duct tape
Phone charger

Some other handy stuff:
Camera
Umbrella/Raincoat
Mosquito Repellant
Baby Wipes (to clean your hands during the day)
Garbage bags (for end of the show clean-up)
Toilet Paper (the Porta-Johns are usually out)
Gloves (for tire changing, etc.)

89.   Call ahead if you are going to be late.

Otherwise, the promoter might give your space away.

Setting up for the show

90.   Use a combination stool/tool box for tools.

If you dedicate a set of tools for shows, and keep them in a combination stool/toolbox, you will always have the tool you need and the stool also helps you put up walls, curtains, and lights at the show.

91.   Keep Band-Aids and ibuprophen in your tool box.

92.   Raise your canopy to its top height.

Your booth will be more inviting and easier for tall people to get into. If you roll up your walls, put them on before raising the canopy.

93.   Use a wagon with large tires for easy loading.

Big wheels roll over cracks better. Magline Gemini carts are the best hand trucks. They have big wheels, 2 or 4 wheel positions and hold up to 800 lbs. Aldens, 800-738-5333 www.handtruckcentral.com

94.   Never put tape on the legs of your E-Z UP.

The sticky residue left will prevent you from closing it down after the show.

95.   Tape the front edge of your rug.

You don't want people to trip on it and sue you.

96.   Take advantage of the show showcase.

Some shows have an area set aside with items from most of the booths, with a label to indicate where the artist is located. Make sure you have something on display.

97.   Don't use "Sale" signs at a fair.

The public expects that the price asked reflects the artist's time and materials. If items are on sale, you have to explain why.

98.   Don't wrap cord around your lights.

Use cable ties to keep your wiring neat. Bring something to cut the ties at the end of the show.

During the show

99.   Write your booth number on your card.

Many people at a show are asking for your card so they can write your booth number on it and come back later to buy.

100.   Show your customers what you start with.

A raw material in the hand is worth a thousand words--wood block, clay ball, metal sheet, etc.

101.   Try to avoid custom orders.

A special order can upset your entire production day. First try to steer them to buying a piece you already have.

102.   Get everything in writing.

If you do take a custom order, both you and the customer should have a copy of the specifications, price, and delivery date.

103.   Get a 50% deposit for custom work.

Full payment in advance is even better.

104.   Never charge extra for gift boxes, etc.

The customer will think you are cheap and resent the charge. Customers like the word "free."

105.   Use one of your walls to close off your booth.

If you have to leave your booth during the show for lunch or bathroom, and no one is around to watch your booth, just put up a wall in front of your booth.

106.   Never criticize other craftspeople.

Nothing looks more unprofessional to customers or other crafters.

107.   No whining about your space.

You might believe yourself and have a terrible show. Or you might get moved to a worse location. Never complain to the promoter unless you are sure it will make a difference for the better.

108.   Tell everyone it is a great show!

When a customer asks you how the show is doing, always say you are doing very well (even if you are having your worst show ever). No one wants to buy from someone who is failing. They figure that if other customers aren't buying, there might be something wrong with your product.

109.   Give a quantity discount.

Customers think they can get a better price if they are buying directly from the artist. But you have to be firm, in case you are dealing with a "flea market" personality. Ten percent is a reasonable amount for three or more items. Don't offer it unless they ask, or you think it might encourage them to buy. Stand firm at ten percent.

110.   Have a book about your craft in your display.

People will browse it while waiting for your attention, and may even assume you are in the book. It adds to the professional atmosphere. An example would be "Fine Woodworker."

111.   Start a mailing list now!

At shows, collect names and addresses with a Guest Book (an address book that lays flat will work. Copy into a database all addresses from the checks you receive. Someday you will have a huge mailing list. At least once a year, send a postcard to everyone on your list, with information about your shows, website, and new products.

112.   Make your own guest book.

Print headings for name, address, phone, and email, horizontally on a sheet of paper, and have Kinko's print it out for you.

113.   Tell people a story about your product.

They want to know what inspired you to make it and how hard it is to make. Have a partially finished work-in-progress to show them.

114.   Tourists buy lower-priced items.

They might be buying for a friend, pet-sitter, someone at the office. Tourists are already spending a lot of money on the trip.

115.   Have signs in your booth that communicate.

Artist's statement, credit card acceptance, discount policy, name of business, etc., all signs that talk to your customers for you. They give customers something to read while you are talking to other customers.

116.   Hide the clutter.

The cash box, VISA machine, your personal items, and bags go under the table. Clutter distracts your customers.

117.   Have a cooler for your water and snacks.

Get free ice from your motel.

118.   Have a trashcan in your booth.

A trash bag clipped under your table helps you keep a tidy booth, and you can take a customer's empty cup and throw it out for them.

119.   Keep your display out of the aisles.

Don't put anything in front of your booth, as it restricts the flow of traffic to the booth next to you.

120.   Bring a roll of good duct tape.

Tape made by Magnum is good. Any tape that says "Duck" is not necessarily good quality.

121.   Make your own sales tax chart.

Use a calculator to calculate sales tax for your best selling items or combination of items and make a list to refer to, so you don't have to recalculate it each time.

122.   Stay in your booth.

If you are bored, take inventory. You won't sell anything when you are not in your booth.

123.   Ask people what they think of your new items.

Do they like the color, the price, shape, etc.? Pay close attention to their comments. This type of feedback is one of the great advantages of doing a retail craft fair or art show.

124.   Include your artist's biography with the purchase.

Some customers will ask you if you have a copy of your "Artist's Statement" to include with their purchase.

125.   Use color postcards instead of brochures.

They are cheaper to make and get the customer's attention.

126.   Never argue with the promoter.

They have enough problems, and you might not get in the show again.

127.   If it can spill, it will.

Coffee and other drink cups always go in a place where, when they spill (not if), nothing will get damaged.

128.   Your chair should be eye-level high.

You shouldn't have to get up to get out of it to talk to the customer. Every time you get up you put stress on your back. You should be able to just slide back into it. The seat should be 30" high. I like Gold Medal canvas chairs and the aluminum chair that www.dickblick.com sells.

129.   Being next to your competition can be good.

Motels and hotels, restaurants cluster together. In Florence Italy all the jewelers are on one bridge. If your competition gets all the sales, you can learn why.

Taking credit cards

130.   Accept MasterCard and VISA charge cards.

People will spend more if they can use a charge card. I use this wireless credit card terminal at shows. It is a "VeriFone" 8000. There are newer smaller cheaper ones. I work with "Total Merchant Services," 888-682-4464. Make sure your machine is set up for "store and forward' when you don't get reception.

131.   Check the customer's credit card for their signature.

If it isn't signed, have them sign it before you take it, then look at their driver's license, and compare the signatures. Some customers prefer not to sign their credit cards. You can't force them to do so, but remind them that a thief could sign their name for them, and then the "false signatures" would match.

132. Never charge extra for charge card usage.

It is illegal to charge a customer extra for using a credit card. However it is not illegal to give a discount for cash.

133. Put up "Credit Cards Accepted" signs.

Some people are looking for this notice, to see if they can still buy from you. They might have run out of cash at another booth.

134. Try to get the customer's phone number.

If you use a manual credit card machine, try to get a phone number and address. It is illegal to require a credit card user's phone number, but you can ask them to put it in your address book for your mailing list. Then you will be able to call them if they left something in your booth.

135. Keep all credit card sales receipts.

Put them in a separate envelope for each show. If the charge is disputed, the signed original will be easier to locate.

136. Bring a manual credit card machine and slips.

If your electric credit card machine fails, runs out of paper, etc, you will still be able to take credit cards.

137. Get charge slips from banks.

If you run out when on the road, go to a local bank for more slips.

138. Always check the slip for clarity.

Check to see if the number and expiration date is clear. Some cards have worn numbers, or the numbers have been tampered with (flattened). Sometimes the machine might not imprint the whole number. When you get home to call the charges in, you won't get paid if you don't have the whole number.

139. Don't charge until product is shipped.

Not only is it against the law, it also puts additional pressure on you.

140.　　Carry a portable battery pack.

Vector (from automotive supply) with a Radio shack 12 volt DC to 110 AC converter, will come in really handy if your credit card terminal battery goes dead. This EverStart is from Target, works okay. Walmart and Sears also has them.

Avoiding theft

141.　　Keep valuables out of reach.

Thieves will reach under your table or in from the back of your booth. Put your purse or camera in a Rubbermaid or a large trunk.

142.　　Shoplifters usually travel in pairs.

One distracts you while the other takes something. Keep your eyes open for unusual questions, or really dumb ones repeated over and over. They ask to see things you don't have out, then when you turn your back, they steal.

143.　　Don't use a cash box.

Keep your money (at least all paper money) on your body, in a pocket, in a fanny pack, etc. You can keep coins in a handy box for sales tax change. It would be noisy when stolen.

144.   Separate large bills from small bills.

Don't keep your money all in one place. Keep large bills in a separate safe place that is harder to access, a different pocket, etc. This keeps you from giving someone big bills in their change, or spilling the money on the ground.

145.   Attach your purse strap to something.

A chair leg, table leg, canopy leg, etc. Purse-snatchers at fairs are looking for a purse that is unattached.

146.   Take your banner down at night.

Thieves won't know which booth is yours.

147.   Don't read in your booth.

Reading is a signal to thieves that you are not watching.

148.   Wear sunglasses at outdoor shows.

This deters thieves, because they don't know what you are looking at.

149.   You are vulnerable to theft when packing up.

You are separated from your stuff when going to the car, and again when the stuff is in the car and you are back at the booth. Lock your car doors anytime valuables are inside.

150.   Don't park far away just to save money.

Items in your booth might get stolen if you don't have anyone watching them, because you are gone longer to get the car.

151.   Insure your inventory.

Check your homeowner's or renter's insurance policy. It might cover your stock. Call the agent and find out how much is covered. Your computer system might be covered as well.

152.   Stash the cash.

Put your money in a safe place as you travel back and forth to your car after the show.

153.   Have a locked storage box or trunk.

A Contico wheeled locker can be locked in your booth with a padlock and bike cable passed through the frame of something heavy. Toss little things like your credit card machine in it for overnight storage. If a drunk or bum gets in your booth at night, they won't get into it.

After the show

154.   Always fill out the show survey.

That is the best way to get the promoters to improve the show. Don't just write your complaints. Give helpful suggestions on how to improve the show. If they don't know what is wrong, how can they fix it?

155.   Always donate an item for the auction.

Many shows have an auction of artworks from artists to raise additional money for the local art organization. This donation may be remembered when next year's applicants are chosen. You don't need to donate your best piece. Often a discontinued style is the perfect choice.

156.   Be in your booth early.

If you spend 60 minutes in your booth before the show is open, it adds up to three extra hours in a three day show. (That is, if you're prepared to help customers during the extra time…) Or, one extra show for every six shows, at no extra cost to you. This applies to outdoor shows with no fence.

157.   Wait 30 minutes after a show ends to pack up.

After 30 minutes, 75 percent of the other artists will be gone and out of your way. If you are rushing to get home after a show when you are tired, you are more likely to have an accident. Plus, you might make a few more sales.

Indoor show survival

158. Put electrical equipment close to the plug.

With long cords, some power is lost due to resistance in the line.

159. Floor coverings make everyone more comfortable.

A 4'x 6' oriental rug in darker colors will make your booth look more elegant and make your feet less tired at the end of the day.

160. Stand on a dishwasher mat.

Big rubber mats are available from restaurant supply dealers. They are good for relieving leg fatigue. Koffler Sales Corp, www.kofflersales.com

161. Bring extra shoes.

Switch between them during the day. Go barefoot for an hour now and then, especially when you are set up on grass or carpet. Use Dr. School's shoe inserts.

162. Use fitted tablecloths.

They also should come down to within 3 inches of the floor.

163. Buy certified fireproof cloth for your tables.

Keep the certificate with you. Then you never have to worry about it, even though they seldom check.

164. Spray your cloths to fireproof them.

The local fire department can tell you where to get Flamort. You spray your tablecloths and let it dry. Keep the empty bottle as proof. Sometimes the fire department will put a match to your cloth to see if it burns. www.flamort.com 510-357-9494

165. Use three-prong grounded plugs everywhere.

Use three-prong grounded cords and three-prong power strips.

166. Be friendly to the craftsperson next to you.

You need friends, not enemies. Avoid negative craftspeople.

167.   Use halogen bulbs.

One 50-watt halogen bulb equals a 75-watt incandescent bulb. If you are allowed 500 watts total, use ten 50-watt halogens for brightness (equivalent to 750 watts from incandescent bulbs). Halogen bulbs also produce better colors.

Outdoor show survival

168.   Bring lots of spring clamps.

Don't expect the zippers to work with your E-Z UP. Home Depot sells big clamps.

169.   Always have a weight handy when you set up.

You should tie your booth to a weight or immoveable object while you are setting up, in case of a gust of wind.

170.   Use a fan in your booth.

A deep cycle battery will power several 12-volt fans to help stay cool. You can get the deep cycle battery at Sears and the 12-volt fans at a truck stop. You can also use a small solar panel on your canopy roof to power your fan. Get an electric fan for shows that provide electricity. Customers will love it, too.

171.   Get other 12-volt accessories at truck stops.

They have 12 -volt coffee makers, coolers, vibrating massaging seat backs, hot plates, etc. You can also get hookups to play your iPod or satellite radio through your cassette CD player.

172.   Try a gray or white tarp under your canopy.

This will make it cooler, stopping the heat from coming in from the top. This applies to the thinner canopy tops.

173.   Freeze water bottles, 7/8 full, at home.

You will have cold water on the road as the ice melts.

174.   Keep a roll of paper towels in your booth.

They're handy for coffee spills and wiping errant rain drops (or dust) off your products. Offer one to a sneezing customer.

175.   Store everything in Rubbermaids.

You will have much more peace of mind during a rainstorm.

176.   Bring a heating pad or blanket.

Handy at cold outdoor shows that have electricity.

177.   Use 8-gallon plastic water cans for weights.

Get the ones with handles (sporting goods stores for campers). Fill them at a gas station or food booth when you get to the show and dump them at the end of the show. 8 gallons of water weighs 65 lbs. The empty cans will save you gas, since more weight in your vehicle lowers gas mileage.

178.   Use your spare tire for an emergency weight.

If you forgot your weights, use your spare tire. Use a rope to attach it to the center or top corner of your booth.

179.   Use barbell weights for booth weights.

Use the hole in them for hanging.

180.   Use 25 lb. dumbbells for booth weights.

They are easy to carry, and you can bungee them to canopy legs. The six-sided ones won't roll around in your car. You can also use them to work out on the road.

181.   Makeshift weights from bags of sand.

Sand is cheap and available from a hardware store. It comes in plastic bags, weighs 60 lbs., and can simply be poured out into a river or garden when the show is over.

182.   Make your own weights with PVC tube.

Fill a 6" diameter PVC pipe, 36" long, with concrete, using end caps and 12" eyebolts with washers. They can be tied to the legs of the canopy (remember, no tape on canopy legs) or fastened to the upper frame with a rope. Florida artists use 100 lbs. on each corner of their display. (It can be very windy in Florida!) Don't use 3" or 4" tube—you'll waste your time on light weights.

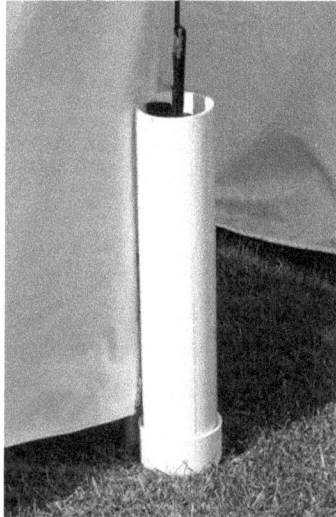

183.   Attach weights to top of tent as well as legs.

Attach the rope to the cross bar on E-Z UPs. When weights are used only on the legs, the tent can still twist in the wind.

184.   Use deck screws to attach canopy to asphalt.

You will need to carry an electric screwdriver. Use 2 ½" screws with a washer. 1 ½" drywall screws will also work. If you don't have washers, use two screws to a hole. You can also use 1 ¼" concrete nails with washers to hold your booth down. They are harder to get out at the end of the show. (Check with the promoter to be sure it is okay to chew up the city's asphalt this way.)

185.   Use metal stakes in hard ground.

E-Z UP canopies come with 12" nail-like stakes. They are designed to be hammered through the hole in each leg plate.

186.   Use a dog stake on grass.

Screw a stake in the ground at the middle of each side and at the back, then tie ropes to each corner. This also keeps the tent from leaning.

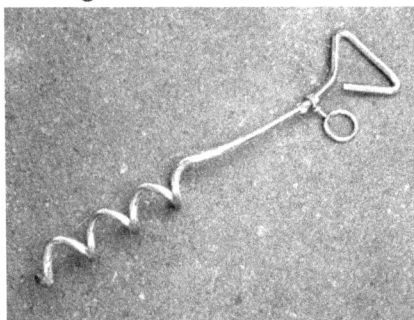

187.   Use clamps to keep the top from pooling.

Old, sagging awning covers allow rainwater to pool. You can douse your neighbors (or the passing public) by pushing the pool up with a broom handle. Or use a clamp on the E-Z UP frame inside to reduce the sag and stop the top from collecting water. Make sure the clamp has the rubber handle covers so it won't tear the canvas.

188.   Bring lots of rope.

You will need rope to tie your canopy to your weights or another booth. You also might tie your booth to a tree, fence, or park bench.

189.   Use a GFI (ground fault interrupter).

Nearly all shows that provide electricity provide a GFI.

190.   Never stand in water when unplugging lights.

Stand on something dry, like cardboard or a ladder.

191.   Keep your outlet dry.

Make sure it is in your booth at night. Raise it up off the ground. Don't wrap a plastic bag around the outlet; it might fill up with water.

192. Keep an ear on the weather.

A weather radio can be purchased at Radio Shack for less than $50. You should ask a customer at the show which county the show is in, as the reports are given by county.

193. Don't let booth lights shine in the customer's eyes.

194. Make an awning for your booth with conduit.

Get three ten-foot pieces of 1" conduit. Clamp two on each side of your E-Z UP, poking out the front about 3 feet. Clamp one piece in the middle. You can fold up a wall, or use a banner, and hang it across the pipes. Put clamps on the ends. Use it in rainy weather or when you are facing the sun. Some of the new Caravan canopies come with an awning. Make sure it is 6' 6" tall or more, so no one bumps their head on it.

195.   Drop your canopy to half height in the wind.

If it is so windy you might lose it, leave it half-height overnight. This cuts your wind resistance and keeps your canopy legs straight. This only works if you don't have high panels holding your artwork in your booth.

196.   If it is really windy take your canopy down.

This is what might happen if you don't.

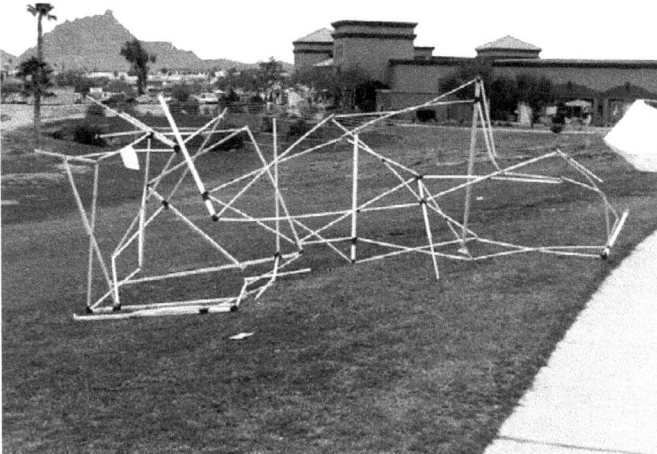

197.   Make sales in the rain.

If your customers can get out of the rain in your booth, then you might make a few extra sales while waiting for the rain to stop.

198.   Don't tolerate really loud music.

When nearby music is too loud and interfering with your ability to converse with your customers, **ask the musicians to turn it down**. Sometimes simply turning a speaker will solve the problem. If that doesn't work, then **ask the promoter to get the music turned down**. You shouldn't have to raise your voice at a craft show to sell your products. You have paid for the right to sell your craft. If the promoter doesn't solve the problem, then don't do the show again and tell the promoter, and the show guides, why.

Selling

199.   Emphasize the benefits, not the cost.

When advertising, tell the customer how they will benefit. Just owning one-of-a-kind art is a great benefit. Function is a benefit. Function helps to sell art. "You benefit by having a 'one-of-a-kind' item and being able to use it to….."

200.   Use the key word, "yes."

Yes, I have a gift box. Yes, I take charge cards. Yes, I have a trash bag. Yes, yes, yes.

201.   Listen to your customers.

They notice if you are not listening. If you are already dealing with a customer, and a second customer interrupts, ask the first customer if you can talk to the second. Deal with the question politely, and then get back with your first customer.

202.   Stay busy during slow times.

Clean up your booth, straighten out your display.

203. Make notes on the back of a business card.

When someone gives you a business card, write down on the back what was discussed: send a brochure, information about a show, make custom order, etc.

204. Suggest the lower priced item.

This will help you get the customer's trust quickly.

205. Offer a hesitant customer a guarantee.

Offer a full refund, replacement, or repair if customer is dissatisfied.

206. Talk to everyone who stops at your booth.

Have enthusiasm for your creations. Others will come over to see what the attraction is. Ask questions.

207. Act less like a salesperson, more like an artist.

Don't pressure your customers.

208. Make your customer feel comfortable.

Offer an extra chair, chocolate, water, whatever it takes.

209. Educate your customer.

Art sales involve 50% education and 50% sales technique. Most people at your booth have no idea how you do what you do. Tell them why your work is special and worth the price. Be prepared to talk your head off. Don't let a few know-it-alls discourage you.

210. Mention environmental aspects of your craft.

If you have an environmental angle to your product, describe it. Conservation of resources is very important to some people. Tell them how you use materials economically. Tell customers about your lifestyle.

211. If people ask for your card, get their address.

Hand them a guest book to write it in. You can mail them a postcard or catalog later. Do this whether you have a business card or not.

212.   Never sell seconds.

They will come back to haunt you, especially if your customer gives them to someone else, who doesn't know they are seconds, and brings them back to you to fix. It is better to have the "Everything I sell is top quality." attitude. People don't want flawed items for gifts.

213.   Never judge a customer by their appearance.

Every artist has a story about the customer who looked like a hobo, but bought a very expensive item.

214.   Put the product in their hands.

Use the sense of touch. Also use smells and sounds. Customers are sometimes too cautious about handling the merchandise. Encourage them to do so, unless it is breakable.

215.   Ask the customer to "Tell me more."

Learn as much about them as you can without being intrusive.

216.   Give each customer personal attention.

Make them feel special. Ask for their name.

217.   Most customers want to be greeted.

Say "Hi," and then leave them alone for a minute. Give them a little time to look around, and then answer their questions clearly.

218.   When the customer is interested, get involved.

Ask, "How can I help you?" "What do you think?" "How many do you want?" "Will these provide a solution?"

219.   Maintain eye contact.

If you are looking all around the show, they will too.

220.   Ask them why they bought your product.

This will help you improve your product. If they didn't buy, ask them why not.

221. Ask customers about their family.

If their children are grown and out of the house, they have more spendable income.

222. Stay in touch with your good customers.

Use your computer to keep a list of everyone who has bought anything for the last five years. Contact them at least twice a year.

223. Remind people if it is the last day of the show.

There are customers at every show who think the show goes on forever.

224. Share information about your craft.

Share enough about how you make your product so someone could make it, but don't give away the special secrets you use to make your product better.

225. Use key words to make sales.

Some comfortable words are "warm, soft, clean, powerful, bigger, better."

Health

226. At the first sign of a cold, take vitamin C.

3,000 mgs a day should keep the cold at bay. Also take a multiple vitamin every day.

227. Take aspirin to thin your blood.

Aspirin is known to reduce strokes and heart attacks.

228. Keep warm.

It is always amazing to me how many artists have no socks on a cold rainy day. Your entire attitude about the show and customers can be related to your cold feet. Or your head. People lose 10% of their body heat through their head. Wear a hat.

229.   Exercise on a regular basis.

30 minutes on a treadmill and lifting dumbbells, three times a week, makes a world of difference on your stamina and attitude.

230.   Stretch every day.

A few yoga stretches every day will help you avoid back pain.

231.   Drink lots of water during a show.

Dehydration will cause headaches and soreness. Don't drink a lot of coffee unless you have a Porta-John nearby. Combat the low humidity of indoor shows with water.

232.   Never eat shellfish before or during a show.

One crafts couple I know spent the entire weekend in the hospital after having a cheap lobster buffet in Las Vegas, and another friend spent Sunday at a big show in Park City lying on his stomach after eating shellfish and peppers at a restaurant the night before.

233.   Wear sandals on hot days.

Remember to put on sturdy shoes when packing up.

234.   Get fumes out of your shop with a fan.

Get an inline duct fan from Armstrong Fan Co., Box 968, Jackson, MI 49201 517-764-2300

235.   Keep your workshop neat for safety.

Keep your workspace neat and clean. Use lots of lighting.

236.   Reduce stress at your workbench.

Sit upright without your head and neck bent forward. Knees should be higher than hips.

Travel

237.   Never drive when sleepy.

McDonald's coffee or Coca Cola will keep you awake! Better to be alive with bad coffee than dead with no coffee.

238.   Keep a travel kit in your car.

A travel kit is a bag with toothbrush, deodorant, toothpaste, floss, and nail clippers, hairbrush, ibuprophen, aspirin, and multiple vitamins. If you keep it in your car or van at all times, you won't find that you have forgotten one of the above when you get to your show.

239.   Keep a small fire extinguisher in your car.

Always carry a fire extinguisher in your car or van. I had an engine fire in a gas station once, and used the fire extinguisher to put it out. Saved my van, my stock, and the gas station!

240.   Use mapquest to get a map to the show.

Usually the show promoter will give directions do the show, but mapquest can also give you directions from the show to your hotel. www.mapquest.com

241.   Always carry jumper cables.

You might leave your lights on and kill your battery. Your friend might need a jump-start. Get 12 guage, not 14 or 16.

242.   Carry a first aid kit.

If you keep a well-stocked kit in your car, you will have what you need to fix a blister or scraped knuckle at the show.

243.   Check your tire pressure.

Carry a tire gauge. Fully-inflated tires can increase your gas mileage 15%. About 5 lbs less than maximum pressure stated on the side of the tire should do it.

244.   Learn how to check your car fluids.

No one else is going to check them for you all the time. Learn where the oil, transmission, power steering, and wiper fluids are filled, and how to check them.

245.   Don't use the cheapest gas at cheap stations.

It might be "flat" because it sits around longer. Flat gas costs you mileage. It also might have water in it.

246. Check if your transmission needs fluid.

If your car is stalling, it might be the transmission. Sometimes a little fluid will get you to the next town or even home. It might be all the transmission needs, and you don't have to get it fixed.

247. Check your steering belt if steering is hard.

See if the belt to the pump is missing. If it is in place and relatively tight, check your power steering fluid. Also, check your front tires. A flat front tire makes steering difficult.

248. Clear your gas line with STP water remover.

Get it at Kragen or Pep Boys. Make sure the bottle says something about water removal from gas lines. Water buildup comes from condensation or fog, and will make your engine run rough.

249. Carry a spare alternator belt.

The service station might not have one if yours breaks. Have someone show you where it is under your hood, so you can know if it is broken. Usually the alternator light will come on. A salesman at NAPA Auto Parts will tell you which one you should use. They are pretty easy to replace, with a wrench and a screwdriver.

250. Carry extra keys.

Keep them in a magnetic case under the car. Kragen sells the case.

251. Get a better price on a used car.

Check the Kelly Blue Book Company for used vehicle price range. www.kbb.com Used cars can be found on www.traderonline.com. If you need a used cube van go to www.ryder.com.

252. Ask for a room away from the freeway.

Quiet rooms are on the other side from the freeway. Ask for a room with unoccupied rooms on either side.

253. Use a solar panel to run your RV lights.

Use a regulator so the battery doesn't overcharge. RV Solar Electric, 14415 N. 73rd st., Scottsdale, AZ 85260 800-999-8520

254. Park your RV at Wal-Mart overnight.

Park in the lot as far from the door as possible. They let you stay one night with no hassle. The legend says that the founder was once without a place to stay. Be sure to buy some stuff from them the next day.

255. Get an AAA or AARP card for a motel room discount.

Either of these cards will save you at least 10%. AARP cards are only available to people age 50 and over.

256. Get a road service for car towing.

The number for AAA is 800-922-8228. Sears Allstate Motor Club also has a good plan and their number is 866-209-0394.. If you have an RV you can get Good Sam Emergency Road Service. 1-800-234-3450. Service includes gas, flat changing, and lockout service.

257. Check your spare tire for air.

You might be driving around with a flat spare tire, which would be no help at all. Check for a car jack and a tire iron. Use the big x shaped tire iron. A woman can use one of these to loosen nuts. Learn to change your own tire; anyone can do it. Sure, AAA can change it, in an hour or so. But you might miss the show. Carry gloves and grubbies to put on to change the tire. And keep a working flashlight. It is usually worthwhile to carry a floor jack if you have room. They are much faster and easier to use than the pneumatic or scissor type.

Theft on the road

258. Don't tell the motel clerk you have valuables.

Don't even ask if they have a lock box, unless it is an extremely reputable motel or hotel chain.

259. Leave a light and TV on in your motel room.

A thief might think it is occupied when you are gone.

260.   Put a lock box in your van or station wagon.

You can get them from the pick-up truck stores, where people buy them to lock up their tools. You can order one to bolt onto your van floor or your trunk.

261.   Lock your trailer hitch.

I know or have heard of at least six artists who had their trailer stolen in a motel parking lot.

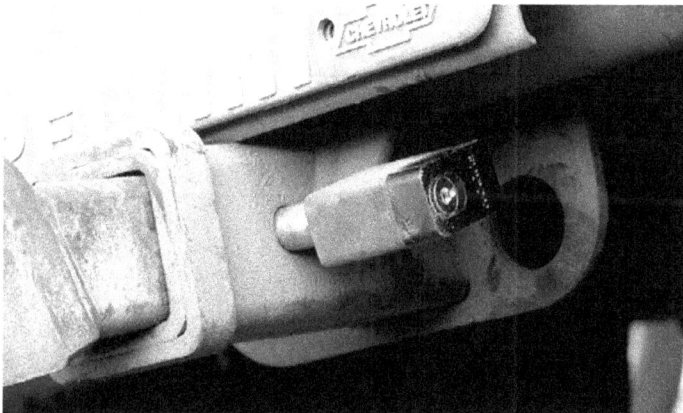

262.   Paint a number on top of your trailer or van.

It should be clear and big enough to be seen from a police helicopter. If the police won't help you find your trailer, you can always rent a helicopter and look for it yourself. Chances are it will be found only a few miles from where it was stolen.

263. Don't leave your key in your car ignition.

Don't leave it in the ignition when you are loading in or packing up, or when your car is in your driveway, or gas station, or anywhere, ever. Also, don't leave your cell phone in plain sight. Thieves will sometimes break a car window just for a cell phone.

264. Use a steering wheel locking device.

If you don't have a burglar alarm, at least get a steering wheel lock. The Club (Le Club) costs about $30, and might save all your stock.

265. Get an alarm with a pager.

You want to know when it goes off, especially when you are on the third floor and can't hear it. With a pager you will know if it is your alarm. An alarm and Le club will cost $200 total; a pager is about $100 more.

266. Your alarm should have an engine kill feature.

If the alarm is tripped, the engine can't be started until the alarm is reset. Even if the thief disconnects the horn or siren, they still won't be able to take your car. Sometimes they break in just for a ride, and don't want your stuff.

267. Avoid false car alarms.

Ask the installer to make sure the alarm will stop and reset itself after 30 seconds, so if the car is only bumped or the switch gets wet or there is a loud noise, it won't keep going off all night.

268. Get a flashing red light with your alarm.

The red light should be on your dash. It tells both you and a thief that your alarm is on. The thief will move on to an easier car.

269. Always park in a well-lit area.

Park in front of your door at the motel, or in front of or very near the lobby. If you have a view of your vehicle, you can see by your flashing lights if the alarm is your car or not.

Flying to a show

270. Book roundtrip flights with www.travelocity.com.

At this time, they seem to be able to locate the best prices for round-trip airline tickets.

271. Use a travel agent to book separate flights.

Use a travel agent if you are flying to one city and returning from another. They can also tell you if you will need a car or not to get from your hotel to the show, and they might find you a room at a pretty good price. A good agent that I use can be reached at 800-835-5090.

272. Book rooms with www.priceline.com.

Offer a ridiculously low price; you just might get it. Start with two and a half stars. You might get bumped up to a three star hotel. Only ask for one area with your first offer. You can't raise your price without changing something, so if you don't get your price you can add another area and then up your bid. Bid two stars if you want a room in an extended stay motel with kitchenette.

273. Print out your online airline and hotel reservations.

Take them with you. Sometimes the hotel or motel computer doesn't get the information.

274. Check your E-Z UP as luggage.

Yes, you can check your E-Z Up at no extra charge. It should be in a sturdy canvas carry bag, with any flapping parts taped with duct tape.

275. Ask for the exit door seats.

You will have more leg room.

276. Use UPS to ship packages to your hotel.

70 lbs. From SF to NY costs $56. $40 if you have daily pickup.

277.   Rent canopies when flying to windy areas.

Rented canopies are well weighted. If your canopy costs $80 each way as extra luggage, then a $160 weighted rental canopy is a good idea.

278.   Use your frequent flyer miles.

To find out more ways to get frequent flyer miles, go to www.mileageworkshop.com.

279.   Make a lightweight table with Abstracta ½" tubes.

Abstracta Structures 800-223-7315   www.abstracta.com. You can use their tubes to assemble portable lightweight tables and cases for jewelry with glass or plastic tops.

280.   Put your valuables in your carry-on bag.

Never leave anything valuable in your checked luggage.

281.   Use a collapsible water carrier for weight.

You can get a 5 gal. collapsible water carrier by Reliance (Winnipeg, Canada, R3H-1A4, or Marin Outdoors). Five gallons of water weighs 45 lbs., but the container weights only two lbs empty. Fill at a faucet (food booths), and borrow a hand truck to carry it to your booth.

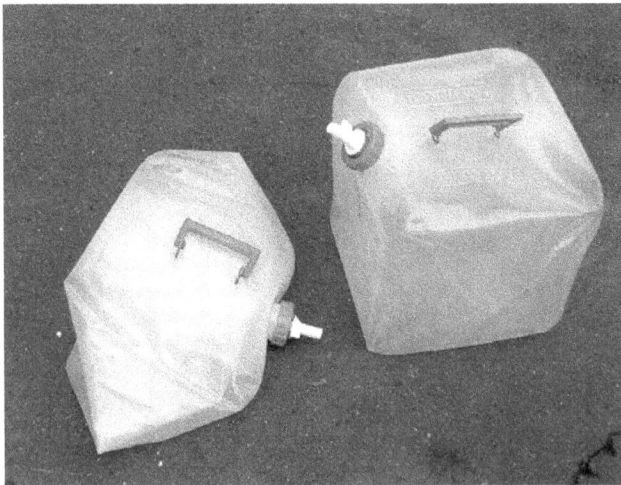

282.   Use concrete blocks for weights.

If you rent a car, get concrete blocks (8" x 8" x 16"), with two holes in them) at the local Home Depot for $3 each, use them for weights, and after the show, give them to another artist, take them back to Home Depot, or leave them in a dumpster or construction site.

283.   Use drinking water jugs for temporary weights.

Tie three 1-gallon water jugs (8 lbs. each) on each leg or eight in the middle. This only works in situations when the weather forecast is good, but is better than no weights at all.

284.   Have a bike lock and cable in your trunk.

A padlock and cable can secure your trunk in case you have to leave it to get a cab, etc. It also helps to have wheels on your trunk.

Wholesale

Wholesale trade shows

285.   Use wholesale shows to help stabilize your income.

You won't have to do as many bad retail shows.

286.   Get on a trade show mailing list.

Philadelphia Buyers Market of American Craft.
Put on by the Rosen Group, 800-43CRAFT.

George Little Management, "Handmade Section,"
 800-272-SHOW www.glmshows.com or
www.glmmarketplace.com. They also put on the New York International Gift Fair.

American Craft Council Shows, 800-836-3470.

287. You have to do a wholesale show several times for it to work.

Gallery owners have to get to know you and trust you.

Trade show booth

288. Get their attention in three seconds.

When a buyer walks by, they scan your booth. They spend up to three seconds deciding whether to visit your booth or not. If nothing is interesting, they will keep walking.

289. Put a banner over the front top of your booth.

Buyers can see over the heads of the crowd to see what you have. You can also put a photo of your product on your banner.

290. Use Zippy Mats for booth floors.

Wandix International, 800-385-6855 www.wandix.com. Stacking interlocking floor rubber pieces, usually 12" by 12", make a comfortable floor in your booth for you and your customers.

291. Attract customers with a drawing.

Have a drawing for one of your pieces. Buyers enter by putting their business card in a bowl. This is an excellent way to get a gallery mailing list. Tell your existing customers about the drawing by postcard.

292. Display fewer items in your booth.

Help your buyer to focus. Reduce the number of samples and colors.

293. Use spotlights on special items.

Use Halogens for jewelry, floods for fiber, par 30's for ceramics.

294. Remove rug wrinkles in front of your booth.

Large halls may put down carpet in the aisles, but sometimes do a poor job. Rug wrinkles cause people to trip. Then they sue. Tell the promoter if there are wrinkles or bumps in front of your booth that you can't smooth yourself.

295. Don't trust security guards.

Security guards don't know how valuable your stuff is. Most of the year they are watching trade show displays, not valuable crafts. Throw a cover over your stuff when you leave. If you catch the guards sleeping, turn them in.

296.   Don't do consignment.

Unless you already have an established relationship with the store, and just want to get rid of a few extra pieces, consignment is probably not a good idea. Most artists and craftspeople don't bother.

297.   Make a double-sided 11" x 17" inch pamphlet.

When folded and stapled, the mailer is 5 ½" x 8 ½". Lots of room for white space, drawings, information, big photos, and an order form.

298.   Make an info display for gallery owners.

Gallery owners need more knowledge about how you make your products. They can display it with your products so they don't have to think about it. The display should have your photo on it, and information about what special techniques you use to make the product.

Shipping

299.   Label every carton you ship to the show.

Labels should include your company name, booth number, name of the show, and name and address of the convention center.

300.   Use a well known shipping company.

Yellow Freight 800-610-6500 www.myyellow.com
UPS 100 weight service, 250 lbs, and $300. 800 pickups
www.ups.com

301.   Track your packages online.

www.packtrack.com tracks UPS, FedEx, and Airborne.

302. Get to know more about the gallery.

Ask the buyer about the gallery location, style, owner's beliefs and preferences. "Where is your store? Do you sell similar crafts? How long have you been in business? Are you involved in management?"

303. Treat gallery owners like artists.

Many of them were (or still are) They are more knowledgeable about your craft than you might think. Don't try to pull the wool over their eyes.

304. Give customers clear bags.

Other shoppers can see what they bought and ask them where they got it.

305. Always wear or use your own product.

Then you will learn how to make it better, or discover whether you should even make it at all.

306. Hand out postcards with your booth number.

When there are hundreds of booths, buyers get confused when trying to find your booth again.

307. Make customers ask for a brochure.

Don't leave them within reach, but in sight. Get the customer's card for each brochure given out. No card, no brochure.

308. If you are not good at selling, bring someone who is.

If you don't know anyone, consider hiring a temp from the local agency.

309. Use a firm handshake.

If your grip is weak, build it up. Squeeze a rubber ball.

310. Get to know your neighbor.

Old timers know where to eat and where to get hardware.

311.   Demonstrate your product.

If there is anything your product does, demonstrate it. If it writes, holds things, carries water, or goes on easy, then you should be showing that all day.

312.   Don't talk down to people.

Go ahead and use big words. They will appreciate it..

313.   Pre-qualify your customer.

Some of the attendees at trade shows do not have stores and are just looking for a good deal. Wholesale buyers have clipboards and are wearing comfortable shoes. Know who you are talking to. Find out from the buyer which other craftspeople at the show they have bought from.

314.   Have a partially made product in your booth.

You can talk about how your product is made, and demonstrate if you have a work-in-progress handy.

315.   Don't sit.

If you act bored, you will be. So will your customers.

316.   Don't smoke or chew gum.

Don't talk on the phone either. It's rude. Make a show of hanging up.

317.   Get plenty of sleep.

Trade shows are hard work, and you need to recover with sleep in order to stay sharp. Party when the show is over

318.   Mercury vapor lighting can cause migraines.

Bring your own aspirins or Tylenol. These lights can also cause a green tinge in your booth. Use halogen lights to improve your lighting and show your colors accurately.

319.   Wholesale buyers are drawn to presentation.

They also like an artist who is well dressed and business-like. Casual dress is for craft shows.

320.   Watch how your customers react.

Give customers a few seconds in your booth before engaging them in conversation. Watch how they react to your designs and prices.

Wholesale show marketing

321.   Attend a show as a guest.

You just have to register as if you have a store. Make notes about booth designs and price points of products similar to yours.

322.   Tell retailers what's new in your booth.

They can always order the old stuff over the phone (even though they usually don't, waiting for you to call them instead!)

323.   Write down buyer comments.

 Eavesdrop on people who are visiting your booth, and write down comments made to you directly. You can study the comments later, to see what you can do to improve your sales.

324.   Don't tell gallery owners what they can sell.

 You don't have to tell them, they already know. Just tell them why your product is better.

325.   Don't print too many catalogs.

Even if a show has 20,000 attendees, only 300 might stop at your booth. You won't need thousands of catalogs.

326.   Don't take more orders than you can handle.

Before a wholesale show, calculate how many items you can make in the next six months. Never promise a delivery date you can't keep.

327.   Make a short DVD or video.

You might want to show customers how you make your products with a video shown on a small TV or a DVD in a portable DVD player in your booth. It should not be longer than 2 minutes. If it is longer, it will distract customers from looking at your products.

328.   Mail postcards before the show.

Pre-show mailings will help you to have a good show. If it is your first show, you might be able to rent the mail list from the promoter, or arrange to have them mail your postcards to their list.

Wholesale business

329.   Get cash for first order.

The buyer can use a check or credit card. No C. O. D. Second order net 15 or net 30. If the retailer wants you to make an exception, such as net 45, they will want exceptions later. If they need net 45, they can use a credit card. If they have a poor credit history, have them send a money order.

330.   Don't ship a new order until last order is paid.

Tell the buyer of this policy when they place their first order.

331.   Don't require big minimum orders.

Large minimum orders discourage small stores. Five of a kind should be enough. You want to get your crafts in stores and keep them in stores. Selling to many small companies is also somewhat safer than selling to just a few large companies. If a large company goes under when owing you money, you could be in big trouble.

332.   Give area exclusivity on a trial basis.

If you commit to exclusivity, the store must make a commitment to sell lots of stuff. Tell your buyer that you will sell to other stores if results are unsatisfactory in their store after three or four months.

333.   Put all terms on the order form.

When buyer signs the order, it indicates that they have read the terms, whether they have or not. But at least you are covered.

334.   Offer buyers a refund or exchange.

Offer them a full refund within 90 days for items that don't sell.

335. Collect past due invoices.

Call and say, "My records show that you owe me xxxx dollars. Will you send me a check for the full amount today?" Letter, phone, letter, phone, letter. Ask for a credit card number to keep until you get the full amount. If you don't get paid, call a lawyer, file a suit.

336. Deliver the order on time.

If you can't deliver the order on time, call the buyer, apologize, and reschedule. When order is late, say, "We did a little extra effort to make sure that you got some unique items."

337. Buy or make a triplicate sales receipts book.

Give one copy to customer at show, one for your files, and one to ship with the order as an invoice. Make sure it has spaces for the delivery date, signature date, contact name, preferred terms, and the customer's signature. If you have a computer invoice program, you only need a duplicate sales book. You copy the information into your invoice program when you get home. I use ProVenture Invoices ($19.95, Office Depot).

338. Make your own wholesale line sheet.

Use 4 pages—one is a photo of crafts, one is terms, warranty, shipping information, one is a price list, one is an artist's statement. Be sure your name, address, phone number, fax, and email address is on every page of material you give the customer.

339. Place a copyright notice on each page.

Put it on every page of your line sheet. (All designs copyright by Joe Artisan Design 2001). Also put the notice on your postcards and everything else you give your customer.

340. Recommend a starter order or show special.

This will help the store get to know your products. Offer a discount of 15% for purchasing the complete starter order. Have signage to describe the show special displayed in your booth.

341. Ask your wholesale customers to reorder.

Call them three times a year. "Hi, I'm _____, from Company. I missed you at the wholesale show. How's your inventory? Can I help you out? Do you need stock? If you want product I have to get you on the production schedule. Do you have any old product to exchange?"

Wholesale reps

342. Get a directory of sales representives.

Directory of Wholesale Reps for Craft Professionals.
http://www.craftassoc.com/olson.html 800-715-9594

343. You can find sales reps at trade shows.

Look for reps with handcrafted items that compliment (but don't compete directly with) yours.

344. Check your sales representative's contacts.

Make sure he or she deals with the type of galleries that sell your type of products.

345. Get references from your sales rep.

Be sure to call the references. Ask them if the rep is reliable, etc.

346. Contract with rep to return your samples.

Some reps think that they should keep the samples. You can make this clear in your contract. The wording should go like this: *We will provide product samples as needed for "selling tools". These samples will be replaced by us when damaged. These samples will remain our property and will be returned at the end of this agreement. These samples have a value of _____ (dollars), and the sales rep shall post a deposit with us for that amount, which will be refunded upon return of the samples in good condition.* From "Microsoft Office for Artists and Craftspeople."

347.   Give only 15% for a rep commission.

The sales rep goes to the store, takes the order, and sends it to you. You ship the order, bill the store, then when the store pays you, you pay the rep 15% of the sale, usually on a monthly basis.

Craft galleries

348.   Sell online at a wholesale website.

www.wholesalecrafts.com is a website for marketing to retailers. You can get a temporary ID and password to view the site by calling Nancy Vince at 888-427-2381 or email nancy@wholesale crafts.com. She says she has more than 500 artists and 5,000 retailers.

349.   Check out <u>American Style</u> magazine.

They have lots of advertising for craft galleries, and you can add the gallery addresses to your mailing list.

350.   Don't just walk into a gallery with your work.

Avoid cold calling. Send photos first, with a cover letter. Get an appointment to meet with the buyer. It shows that you are a professional.

351.   Visit galleries when traveling.

Get the business cards of galleries that could be a match for your products. You never know when these cards can come in handy.

352.   Get postcards from Modern Postcard.

Use www.modernpostcard.com, 800-959-8365. The 4" x 6" size is adequate, or you can get 6" by 8" for a bigger impression. Another good company that I use is www.printingforless.com.

353.   Send a yearly mailing to galleries.

Send postcards to galleries that you have visited in person or that sell crafts that compliment yours.

354.   Make a gallery mailing list.

Your local library has every telephone Yellow Pages in the country on microfische. Look for craft galleries, museums, or gift shops, and write down the address. There is a list of 1100 galleries at www.craftshowplace.com.

Internet

Selling on eBay

355.   List on Thursday for 10 days.

You will have two full weekends for people to see your product. The listing will end on Sunday, when people are home. If you list in the evening, more people will be home to bid as the auction closes.

356.   Use low-res pictures.

Resize your digital pictures to 4"x5" at 72 dpi with Elements or Photoshop. Have a separate folder on your computer for your eBay photos. You can use a film camera and have your pictures delivered on a cd, or buy a cheap 3.2 megapixel camera with a macro lens for under $150.

357.   Use your artist's statement for "About Me."

You can cut and paste your artist statement to eBay, to help your customers get to know you better.

358.   Use bulleted text in description.

Customers don't want to read large blocks of text.

359.   Be descriptive!

eBay does not charge more for long descriptions. You can go into great depth about how you make it, what materials you use, and how successful you are at shows.

360.   Use Turbo Lister for multiple listings.

It is a free program from eBay. You can choose from hundreds of templates, use the same shipping information for all listings, and upload all of your listings at once. You can schedule listings for later automatic uploading.

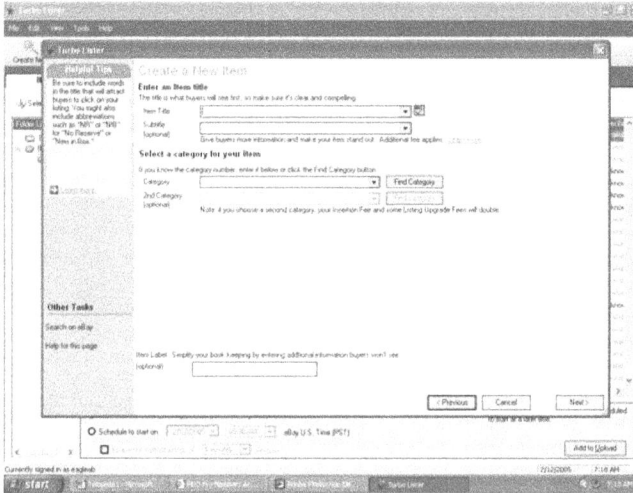

361.   Take PayPal for faster sales.

You have to get set up for PayPal, at www.paypal.com. This service is almost indispensable for internet transactions. Don't forget that cookies must be active to use it on your computer.

362.   Build good feedback on eBay.

You can build up positive feedback by buying inexpensive items and paying quickly. You need 10 feedbacks to sell quantity items

Making your own website

363. Use a white background on your web pages.

Have you ever tried to read white text on a black background?

364.   Use FrontPage for Windows.

FrontPage costs under $125.00 and is easy to learn. Get the book *FrontPage in 24 hours*.

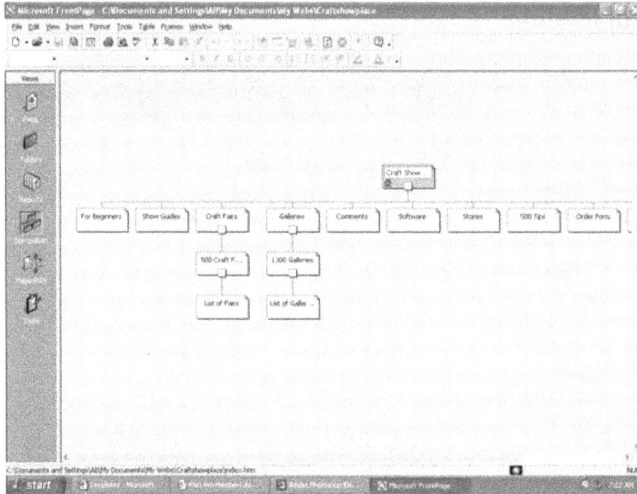

365.   Study bad web design.

Learn what make for bad web design, and avoid it. Go to www.webpagesthatsuck.com. Really!

366.   Don't use fancy animation or music.

It takes too long to download. There are zillions of people out there who still have a slow connection.

367.   Get your own domain name.

You can register your domain name at www.networksolutions.com. It is always better to be in control of your domain name, so you will be notified directly if it is going to expire.

368.   Get listed with search engines.

Most Search engines use the first 12 or 15 words of text on your page. Make them relevant. Don't waste them on "Welcome to my home page." Go to "add url" buttons on Yahoo, Google, or Exite to add your site.

369.   Find a good Internet Service Provider

The ISP (web host) that I use is http://www.linuxwebhost.com They charge $100.00 a year, and have all the FrontPage extensions, so you don't have to worry which version of FrontPage you use. They have excellent and fast customer service. Check out their website.

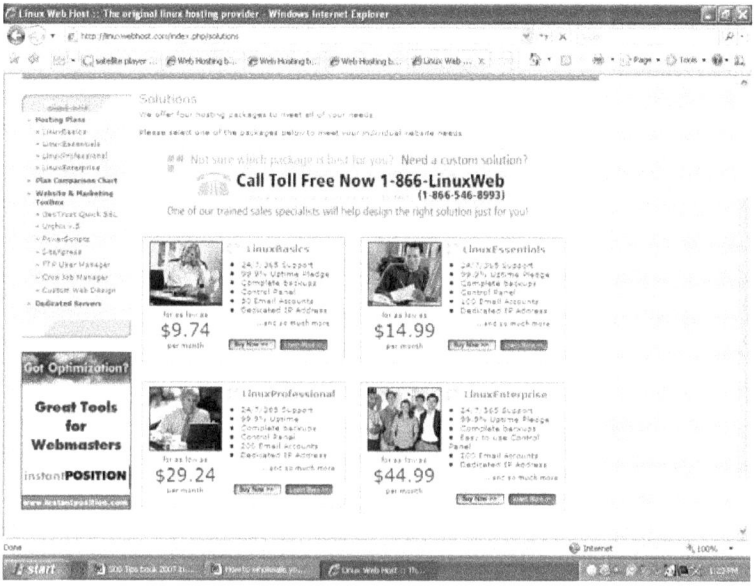

370.   Always use metatags.

Use metatags on all of your pages. In your HTML view, insert them after the title. Example: <META NAME="Keywords" CONTENT="wood, box, handmade, handcrafted, oak, gift, unique"> <META NAME="Description" CONTENT="Handmade wood boxes make excellent gifts for all occasions.">

371.   Don't list your craft shows on your site.

New artists in your medium will apply to all of your shows, get in some of them, and either take your place or half of your money in sales. This has happened to me twice. The huge loss of money hardly compensates for the occasional customer who went to your site to see where you were going to be next. You can send your best customers cards or email them about your upcoming shows.

372. Make a separate page for wholesale customers.

To put wholesale prices on your site, just make a page called yoursite.com/wholesale.htm, and tell your stores about it. Your retail customers won't know it is there.

373. Your web images should be 50K or less.

FrontPage has a feature which shows how long a page will take to download on slow (28kps) connections. Use Adobe Elements or Photoshop to resize your photos. Resize photos to 5"x7" at 72dpi.

374. Make your pages download fast.

Test your success. When downloading your web page, hold your breath. If you can't hold it until the page is downloaded, the page is too big.

375. Have a separate email address.

If your email is connected to your website and it goes down, you won't get any mail. You also get lots of junk mail, which sometimes fills your box, and then you won't get your business email.

376. Don't use free website hosting.

Free hosting has banner ads. It looks very unprofessional.

377. Make an order form page.

Order forms are not hard to make. You can make a form from scratch with FrontPage in a few minutes. Select Insert, then Form. Be sure to right-click on the form you have made and select "form properties" to make sure it goes to your email address. Once you learn a little about order forms, you can copy one from another website, then paste it on yours and make changes. Try the one at www.craftshowplace.com.

378.   Use free PayPal shopping cart.

At www.paypal.com, you can get either "buy now" buttons for each product, or a shopping cart for all of your products. It is easy to set up, and free. You just describe the item at the PayPal merchant site, then cut and paste the code in your html view to create a button next to the product. PayPal handles the rest, giving the customer a receipt and putting the money in your account.

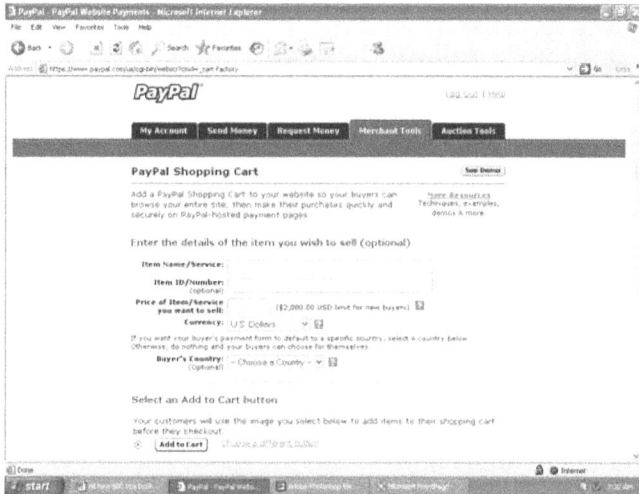

379.   Ask for a verification number.

When taking a phone order, ask for the cvv2 card verification number on the back of the card. Even if you don't use the number, the fraudulent card user won't know this, and won't have one.

380.   Get an email address of everyone who shops.

When they put their email in your address book, they are giving you permission to email them. You can use this email list to notify customers about new products or craft shows. Only do this twice a year, and remove any customers that don't want email from you.

381.   Get free website design from college students.

Contact a local college to find a student website designer who needs exposure. They might be willing to help you for free.

382.   Offer a money-back guarantee on website.

The biggest problem with selling on a website is credibility in the eyes of the buyer. A guarantee will ease their concerns.

383.   Consider a reliability seal.

Check out the Better Business Bureau online to see if their reliability seal would help your business. You have to be a BBB member to get one, and it might cost you $600 or more. www.bbbonline.com

Other Markets

384.   Sell to QVC Shopping Channel.

If you have enough production for $20,000 orders, contact them at www.qvcproductsearch.com

385.   Sell to department store chains.

Contact the store nearest you and get the name and number of the buyer for your region.

386.   Craft malls offer artists more money.

At craft malls, artists pay a fixed amount each month ($30 to $200) for rent, plus a percentage of sales (10%).

387.   A craft mall gives you exposure.

You have the use of a permanent space to exhibit your crafts, without having to run a store.

388.   Sell to craft mall chains.

Cape Cod Crafters has 15 stores, www.capecodcrafters.com
American Craft malls has 7 stores, www.procrafter.com

389. Sell innovative crafts to museum gift shops.

Museum Store Association has a trade show for museum gift shop buyers. www.museumdistrict.com 303-329-6968.

390. Sell traditional crafts at Renaissance faires.

You will need a product without modern day design or components. You will also have to build a "period" booth. This is not a dedicated shopping crowd, though, and you should be prepared to entertain them to get them interested.

391. Sell at county fairs.

If you want to do county fairs, this is the site to find them: International Association of Fairs and Expositions. http://www.fairsandexpos.com/

392. Write articles for extra income.

"Making $$$ at Home: Over 1,000 editors who want your ideas, know-how and experience." Darla Sims, Sunstar Publishing Company, 800-532-4734 amazon.com (search for Darla Sims)

393. Sell your products to catalogs.

Read "Secrets to Marketing your Products to Catalogue Companies" by Jack Briscoe, Jr. **www.gcwoodworks.com** Lots of catalogs are listed at www.catalogsfroma-z.com. A good catalog to check out for handcrafted gifts is www.femailcreations.com.

394.   Open your own craft gallery.

First, add up all of the starting costs you can think of, then calculate operating costs for 6 months. This includes advertising, rent, phone, decorating, etc. If you have this amount of money in the bank, and it is not needed for anything else, then you can consider opening a craft gallery.

395.   Never pay to be in a catalog.

Some mail-order companies promise to print lots of catalogs with your product in them and mail them, and charge you upfront for the printing. Once you have paid the printing costs, what incentive do they have to mail the catalogs? I put my products in a catalog out of Oregon that said they mailed 400,000 copies. I paid them $2500 and got about $300 in orders.

General Business

Bookkeeping

396.   Use a Dome Simplified Monthly Bookkeeping Record.

You can get a Dome book (DOM 612) at Staples, 800-378-2753. You simply enter monthly expenditures on the left, income on the right, and add up the totals at the end of the year or tax time.

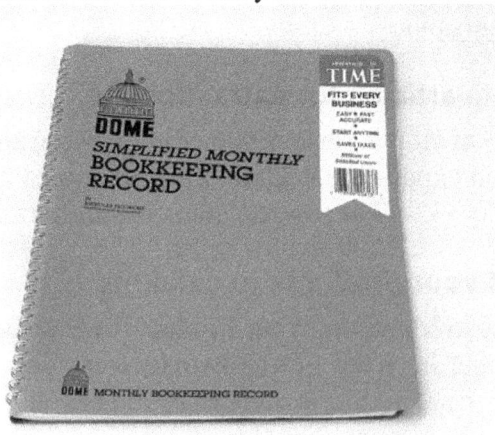

397.   You don't need separate account numbers.

If the item is deductible, write it down in your Dome book. All that is needed for a deduction is a date, item, and amount (and a receipt).

398.   Use QuickBooks if you have employees.

If you don't have at least 3 employees, use a Dome Book instead.

399.   Use basic receipt books.

Use a rubber stamp with your company name and address, phone number and email. Don't bother with the cost of getting them printed.

400.   Don't waste time on fancy forms.

Gallery buyers are not impressed with your sales forms and invoices, but by timely delivery and fast turnovers.

401.   Fill out your phone orders by hand.

You will never have to hate your computer for not booting up in time to take the order. And, you won't have to hate your printer for not working when you need it. Non-cooperative computer hardware has wasted millions of hours of precious time.

402.   Back up your mailing list.

Keep duplicates (including account information) in a place separate from your workplace or office. In case of fire, you won't have to recreate everything. Keep advertising materials in the separate place as well.

Taxes

403.   You have to pay taxes if you have a business.

The IRS considers a business as any activity that creates a profit in 2 out of 5 years. If you don't make a profit, it is a hobby.

404.   Get a sales tax number or ID from your state.

Write, call, or go to the state office of taxation.

405. Get a separate checking account for your business.

The IRS needs to see that you indeed have a business, that you are deducting expenses, and keeping good records of your deductions. A separate checking account also shows your suppliers that you have a business.

406. Find out what is deductible.

The Schedule C tax form has a list of deductions. A Dome book also has a list of everything that is deductible. The bottom line is, if you use it to assist your business, deduct it.

407. Get a fictitious name statement from the county.

If you use any other name than your own name, you need a fictitious name statement. Your bank will usually want one to open your business checking account. You get this from the county office. You have to publish your fictitious name in a local paper for a few weeks. You cannot use your name with a company name, unless you are a company. For example, you can't use Jon Smith Company without registering it, but you can use Jon Smith without registering.

408. Buy supplies in December.

You will be able to deduct them on that year's taxes.

409. Check if a "Home Occupation" business license is required.

In most cities, even if you don't have employees, you might still need a business license to work out of your home. If you have employees, or the public comes to your studio, you will need to have your studio in a commercial zone.

410. Don't deduct permanent items.

A permant item has a useful life of two or more years.

411. Deduct your meals.

When you are on the road, 50% of your meals are deductible.

412. Hire your family and save taxes.

You can deduct the money you pay your children to help, and they don't have to pay taxes on income under $4,300 a year. You don't have to pay Social Security or Medicare for your child under 18 who works for you.

413. Deduct craft books and magazines.

Any safety gear is deductible. Also deductible is tax preparation and advice.

414. Get an employee identification number.

If you have employees, you need an employee identification number (EIN) from the IRS. 1-800-829-4933.

415. Use your social security number.

If you don't have employees, you can use your social security number for business purposes. If your bank requires an employee identification number (and you don't have employees), you can still get one from the IRS. Tell them you want the number "for identification purposes only." Ask for IRS publication 554.

416. Save taxes by using independent contractors.

Independent contractors use their own tools, do the same work for other people as they do for you, and work at their own place or own time schedule. Bookkeepers and shippers are examples.

417. Get free tax information from IRS.

Get IRS publication 334 "Tax Guide for Small Business."

418. Track your bank deposits.

In a field audit, the IRS will add up your bank deposits for the year and compare them with your stated income.

419. Don't deduct for business use of your home.

Since this is the most abused tax deduction, it is a red flag for the IRS, and the deduction (usually a percentage of the rent for a room in your house) is not large enough to be worth it.

420.   Consider an LLC (limited liability corporation).

This business structure limits your personal liability for your business, with less paperwork. If you use the flow-through type, all you have to do is file a Schedule C, the same as you would for a sole proprietorship.

Copyright

421.   Copyright your work.

Copyright costs $45.00 and protects the graphic or sculptural works for 70 years after the artist's death. Copyright forms are free and available from Library of Congress, US Copyright Office. 202-707-9100. Their general information number is 202-479-0700. www.lcweb.loc.gov/copyright.

422.   Get a design patent.

You can't get a design patent for anything that has been in public view for over a year. A design patent is good for 14 years and costs $25.00.   www.uspto.gov 202-707-9100

423.   Copyright your catalog with a "Visual Arts" form.

All of your designs will be protected for your life plus 70 years. www.loc.gov/copyright. Call it a "collection."

424.   Use a "TM" after your company name.

Do this even if you haven't registered the name yet, but intend to.

425.   If someone is copying you, let him or her know.

Tell them that under the law, you are entitled to their profits. They might not even know they are copying you.

426.   Always put a copyright notice on your work.

"Copyright Bob Smith, 2005". The date refers to the first use of your product. Also copyright your catalogs.

427.   Search trademarks online for free.

Go to www.uspto.gov There is a filing fee of $325.00 to register your trademark.

428.   Protect function with a utility patent.

You can't copyright function but you can protect it. Utility patents are good for 18 years. www.uspto.gov.

Using credit cards

429.   Pay your credit card bill immediately.

Pay them the day they arrive in the mail to avoid late fees. If you can't pay it off, at least pay the minimum payment plus 50%.

430.   Deduct credit card interest.

Your business credit cards don't have to be in your business name. Just earmarked for business use. All of the interest on a business credit card can be deducted on your Schedule C. You should use your credit card for materials only if you can pay it off in three months.

431.   Get a credit card that has frequent flyer miles.

You can use them to cut costs for shows you fly to. I use United.

432.   Read the fine print with balance transfer.

If you are late with only one payment, your interest rate can go from 4% to 28%.

Insurance

433.   Get a Homeowners Policy Endorsement.

Your homeowner's policy probably covers business equipment up to $2500. You can raise business equipment coverage from $2,500 to $5,000 for only $25. Check on a homeowners liability endorsement.

434. Get an In-Home Business Policy.

An in-home business policy provides more comprehensive coverage for business equipment and liability than a homeowners policy endorsement. Some will pay for lost income.

435. Consider a Business Owners Policy (BOP)

A BOP covers both property and liability insurance in one policy on a broader scale. Shop around for coverage options and price.

436. Get disability insurance for self-employed.

Start with the Insurance Information Institute www.iii.org It is harder to get in recent years, and may be too expensive to be worthwhile. Some states offer it to individuals, but they don't advertise it. Do a Google search for State Disability Insurance.

437. Open a Medical Saving Account (MSA).

A Health or Medical Savings Account is a tax-exempt account with a financial institution in which you accumulate savings to pay for medical expenses. You can contribute the amount of your current insurance deductible. At age 65, unused MSA/HSA money can be withdrawn for non-medical reasons without penalty (similar to an IRA, ordinary income tax will be charged on the money withdrawn for non-medical reasons). www.msabank.com

Using a computer

438. Get a PC-compatible computer.

If you already have a Mac, fine, but if you are starting out, get a 1-gigabyte or faster PC computer with 256k memory, 50gb hard drive, modem, CD-RW, and Windows XP Home installed. Windows computers are easier than Macs to use (Sorry, Steve, but it is true). You can't run Publisher or FrontPage on a Mac, and you will be dependent on website designers and printing companies.

439. Use Adobe Elements for your photos.

Elements is free with some printers and scanners. It is all you will need to retouch photos and size them for your website or email.

440.   Use Microsoft Works for mailing list.

Microsoft Works costs about $50, and has a word processor, spreadsheet, and database. It is very easy to use for both your word processing and mailing list. I routinely print out 1500 labels, and Works is much easier to use for this than my Office products. Any version of Works after 4.5 will work. In later versions use "print preview" to see labels. If you have Microsoft Office, you can use Excel for your mailing list and Word merge to print the labels.

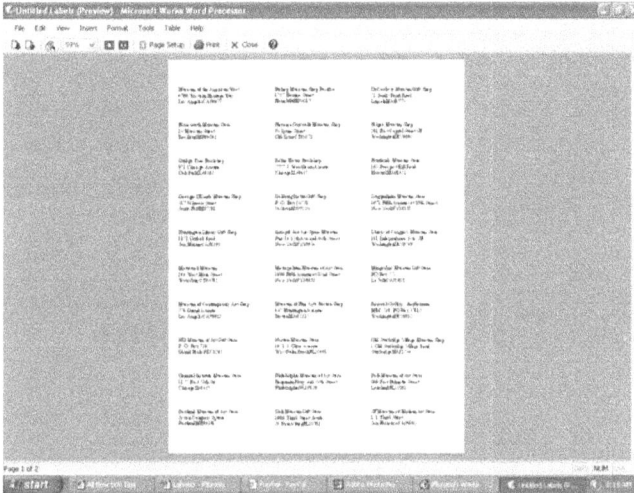

441.   Use Microsoft Publisher for postcards.

Microsoft Publisher is very useful for artist statements, postcards, stationery, catalogs, brochures, hang tags, etc. Some printers such as www.printing4less.com will use your uploaded Publisher files.

442.   Use AOL for your email.

There are lots of so-called free email providers, Yahoo and Hotmail to name a couple. But AOL has reliability, and some neat email tricks, such as being able to unsend your email after it has been sent. I have used AOL since 1995 and have never lost any mail due to "box filled up," etc. If you use full featured AOL from your ISP, it is $15.00 a month. AOL mail is now free.

443. Spend less time on a computer.

The less time you spend on a computer, the more time you have to be creative. Don't get so focused on computers and software that you forget about the customer and making what he or she wants.

444. Try specialized software for artists.

Check out www.workingartist.com. They will send you a free demo of their program with mailing list, invoicer, show organizer, etc

445. You don't need accounting software.

Millions of craft businesses thrived before computers. Do you really need monthly financial statements? You already know if you are not making enough money. Save the time and energy required to learn accounting software. Instead, use it for making new designs, applying to new fairs, and making more products.

General Marketing

Advertising and promotion

446. Place ads in a magazine at least three times.

Six times is better. The customer has to feel they recognize you before they order. Name recognition takes time.

447. Ask for top right corner of a page.

When advertising in print media, remember how the eye travels across the page, then upper right down to lower left, than back across. Like a Z.

448. Pick up newspapers at every show you do.

Take one home with you. Next year, send them a press release. People will come up to your booth and say they saw you in the paper.

449.   Make your own press release.

A press release is one or two pages of information. Tell who, what, where, why, when, etc. Explain why your method or style of craftsmanship is unique or what you are doing to save the planet.

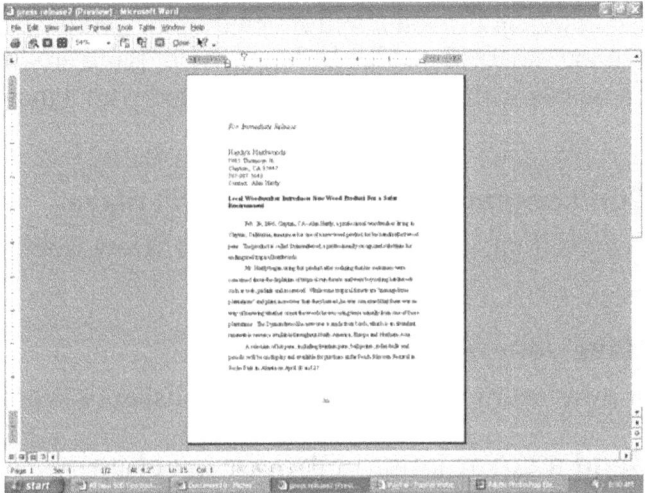

450.   A press release is always double-spaced.

Write "For Immediate Release" at the top, then put your contact information. Three # signs centered at the bottom signals "the end" to the editor, like this: # # #. (I don't know why "the end" wouldn't work just as well.)

451.   Send a cover letter with your press release.

Tell the editor why their readers need to know about you. Include a glossy black-and-white 5x7 or 8x10 photo photograph of you and your shop and a photograph of your craft. You should take the photos in color in case you ever need color, then print them in black and white. (You can't print color from a black and white photo.)

452.   Never write on the back of a publicity photo.

It can't be reproduced, as the writing will show through. Write or use a rubber stamp on a label, then put the label on the back of the photo.

453.   Subscribe to leading craft magazines.

You need to be well informed so you can inform your customers.

454. Join a professional organization.

They usually have a magazine. For example, American Association of Woodturners. (612) 484-9094 aaw@rtpnet.org

455. Personalize your product with engraving.

Engraving equipment is available from engravers who have converted to computer and have old mechanical equipment lying around. Engrave on metals with a diamond bit, and wood with a motor and cutter bit.

456. Don't engrave anything you don't make.

You might mess it up, then what would you do? How would you replace it?

457. Make your own stationery.

Make your own letterhead with Microsoft Publisher or Word.

458. Send a cover letter with your brochure.

Tell the gallery what you sell, what galleries currently have your work, and your prices.

459. Get prints made from your best slides.

Keep them on file for gallery solicitation, and for the few fairs that jury from photos. Send craft galleries prints, not slides.

460. Put what you sell on your business card.

The customer will be reminded what the card is for, or what they saw at the show. I personally don't use business cards at a craft fair, but encourage people to "buy it now," as every thing I make is uniquely different and feels different.

461. Use first class mail for mail order.

Bulk mail only saves you about ten cents a letter. It is more likely to be unread. After you spend $125 for a bulk mail application, $125 for an annual fee, and all the time to separate your mail by zip code, have you really saved any money? Bulk mail rates are at www.usps.com/directmail/

462.   Order smaller quantities of brochures.

If your work changes frequently, you don't want to be stuck with 2,000 outdated brochures.

463.   Attach a photo to your promotional postcards.

If a show supplies you with cards, attach a photo of your latest creation. Print it on label paper and stick it to the postcard that you then mail to your best customers before the show. Be sure to note your name and space number prominently on the card.

464.   Learn this year's colors.

You can learn the colors that are "in" this year by joining the CMG, Color Marketing Group. www.colormarketing.org. Or you can save $715 and just look at what colors wealthy women are wearing.

Pricing

465.   Calculate your selling price.

Labor, plus materials, plus 25% overhead and profit, plus 15% selling fee (sales rep/wholesale expense) times two is your retail selling price.

466.   Cut your costs to reduce your price.

If your price is too high, you might be spending too much for materials.

467.   Raise the price of a slow seller.

If you are not selling a product, and it is reasonably priced, try raising the price.

468.   Selling out is not always a good thing.

If your product sells out the first day, it was priced too low.

469.   You can always give a customer up to 5% off.

Give discounts only if they ask and only after you explain why your product is better. If you have calculated the right price for your craft, you don't have to give discounts.

470.   Never under-price your work.

You might make more sales, but you will be broke at the end of the year. Never reduce your price unless you can cut your costs (both materials and labor).

471.   Drop the styles that are your worst sellers.

There is a business rule that 20% of your products will generate 80% of your income. Believe it.

472.   Don't lower prices at Christmas.

People plan to spend a certain amount on gifts. They don't like to spend less, thinking the person will not appreciate the gift. If you need a less expensive product, make one.

473.   Find your best market.

If your product price is too high for your market, find another market. Do shows in affluent areas. You can sell your one-of-a-kind pieces to a gallery, where your product won't be compared to products at Target or Wal-Mart.

474.   Have multiple price points.

If you have crafts priced for low income, middle income, and high-end customers, you will always make money at a show.

475.   Make holiday gift items under $40.

These could be fun products, whimsical. Then you will make money all year long.

476.   Give promoters a big discount.

You are lucky if a promoter shops at your booth. Treat them well. Also give your friends and relatives, as well as other craftspeople, a discount. They will brag about your product to others, and be a source of free word-of-mouth advertising and good will.

Planning

477.   Make a calendar for the entire year.

Put every show on it, for quick reference.

478.   Sort your deadline schedule.

Using a spreadsheet, make three columns. The first is for the name of the show, the second is the deadline date, and the third is the show date. List your shows, then sort the second column to see which show deadline is coming up next.

Fair	Deadline	Date
Stockton	December 31, 2004	April 22-24
Gaithersburg	January 2, 2005	November 17-20
Lincoln Center	January 4, 2005	Sept. 3-4, 11-12
Columbus	January 5, 2005	June 2-5
Broadripple	January 8, 2005	May 21-22
Boardwalk Virginia	January 15, 2005	June 16-19
Omaha	January 19, 2005	June 24-26
St. George Utah	January 31, 2005	March 25-26
Tubac	January 31, 2005	March 24-26
Mann Arts	January 31, 2005	June 18-19
Portland Arts	January 31, 2005	June 17-19
Half Moon Bay Punkin	February 1, 2005	Oct. 15-16
Palo Alto	February 1, 2005	Aug. 27-28
Pleasanton	February 1, 2005	September 24-25
Minnesota Crafts	February 1, 2005	June 24-26
Utah Arts Festival	February 4, 2005	June 23-26
Penn Sidewalk	February 4, 2005	July 14-17
Three Rivers	February 4, 2005	June 3-19
Strawberry Festival	February 15, 2005	May 14-15
Salem	February 19, 2005	July 15-17
Park City	February 28, 2005	Aug. 6-7
Ann Arbor	February 28, 2005	July 20-23
Kansas	March 1, 2005	June 10-12
Tuscumbia, Alabama	March 1, 2005	June 25-26
Gilroy	March 3, 2005	July 29-31
Cleveland	March 4, 2005	June 17-19
Bellevue	March 4, 2005	July 29-31

479.   Write down a goal for production each day, then do it.

You can do this last thing in the evening, or first thing in the morning.

480.   Inventory your stock and finished products.

Inventory your stock four times a year, not just the once a year that the IRS recommends.

481.   Keep a notebook to record procedures.

Also keep a design notebook. Leonardo da Vinci is said to have filled more than 1,000 notebooks.

482.   Focus on one business direction.

If you are working in two (or more) business directions, make sure you have the time to make them both work.

483. Save money for slow times.

Savings will get you through the highs and lows of craft sales. You should have 6 months living expenses set aside for emergency.

484. Save 10% of the gross from every show.

This adds up. Don't spend it on anything. Save it for your retirement.

485. Open a Roth IRA.

Open a Roth IRA. Maximum Roth annual contribution is $3,000. The income that a Roth IRA account earns is tax-free when you get it at retirement.

486. Don't do slow shows.

If 80% of your income is from 50% of your shows, drop the slow ones and try to get in different (bigger or better) shows.

487. Write down where you want to be in 5 years.

Make goals for 3 months, 1 year, and 5 years. The simple act of writing it down programs the subconscious to take actions that head toward your direction.

Packaging

488. Create hang tags to indicate where the item is made.

They should also show materials used, care and maintenance, and something about the artist. Put environmental issues on your hang tag. If you are doing something to save the planet, tell people.

489. Offer gift-wrapping, when you are not busy.

You will be providing a solution to a customer's problem.

490. Improve your packaging.

Improve your packaging and you will improve your sales. Rio Grande, 7500 Bluewater Rd. N. W. Albuquerque, NM 87121. 800-545-6566. They have packaging and display for small products.
.

Miscellaneous

491. Test market every new product.

That is what craft fairs are good for.

492. Take an art class at a local college.

It will help you to keep your art fresh and avoid burnout. It can be completely unrelated to your craft. When you see how many people want to be artists, you will feel grateful that you already are one.

493. Become an expert in your medium.

Learn everything you can! Take lots of notes. Write a book about what you do. Read new books by others in your medium.

494. Set business hours for your home business.

Self-discipline is the hardest part of being self-employed.

495. Don't listen to negative advice.

It is your business and your art. You can still be open to constructive advice, but cut off any put-downs.

496. Spend your time in your shop wisely.

Find out what wastes time. Use a message machine that says you are in the shop.

497. Get inexpensive legal advice.

Volunteer Lawyers for the Arts is a good starting point for legal advice. There are branches in every state. For a list go to http://dwij.org/matrix/vla_list.html

498. Get a grant.

National Endowment of the Arts, www.arts.endow.gov, has a list of recent grants. You could get money to make a video of your techniques, for example.

499. Get free marketing tips from the SBA.

Check out the Small Business Association www.sba.gov. You can get marketing tips, loans, and sample business plans.

500. Donate some of your proceeds to charity.

Give back. If you want, take credit, and put on your hang tag "5% of the proceeds of this sale to benefit…"

Conclusion

I hope these tips are useful to you in your craft business. I know you won't use all of them, and some of them may seem silly or obvious, but I am confident that there are tips here that probably never occurred to you, that can save you lots of time and money (or at least save your booth).

Please feel free to contact me with any comments about the contents of this book. If you have some good tips of your own, I will include them in subsequent editions of this book, with your permission of course. My email address is eagleab@aol.com.

A good site for lists of shows and galleries, craft fair stories, as well as software for craftspeople, is www.craftshowplace.com.

Good luck with the shows!

Order Form

Microsoft Office for Artists and Craftspeople   0-9655193-1-7 $39.95
This book and CD has over 55 templates and spreadsheets for managing your business if you expand, including templates for pricing your craft, fair deadline organizer, accounting, trade rep agreement, employee applications, non-competing agreement, credit applications, budget, starting your own gallery, project bids, and letter templates for bad checks and other business letters.

---

500 Tips for Marketing Your Crafts   ISBN 0-9655193-6-8   130 pages, $29.95

This is the book you have in your hand. You already know how useful it is. Order copies as gifts for your friends, students, etc.

How to Put On a Great Craft Show   ISBN 0-9655193-8-4   68 Pages, $29.95
Have you ever thought about putting on your craft show? This book will help you make your first show and every show a lucrative event! All the information you need to organize an exciting craft fair or art show is here!   By Lee Spiegel

---

To order any of the above publications, send a copy of this form and a check for the total amount of the order plus $4.95 for Priority Mail shipping to Craftmasters, P. O. Box 1655, Sebastopol, CA 95473. California residents add 7% sales tax. Allow up to a week for delivery. MasterCard, Visa, and AMEX also accepted. You can also order online at www.craftmasters.com

Quantity	Title	Price	Total
Name:		Sub-Total:	
Address:		Shipping:	$4.95
City, State, Zip:		California Tax 7%:	
Email:		Total:	
Phone:		-----------------------	----------
Card Number:		Expiration Date:	
Signature:		-----------------------	----------

Alive again!
       an' ready to show
Winter's over
       I'm rarin' to go

Goodby to the boredom
       dull staring at walls
Now I am Faire-bound
       off to the Malls.

Ol' Bertha is flying
       past princes and prole's
Filled to the sunroof
       with pitchers and bowls

So scatter before me
       you freeway turtles
I am a Red Streak
       bounding hurdles.

Friends and Fortune
       beckon ahead.
Bright lights, warm smiles,
       and plenty of bread.

I come once again
       to hear the praise,
Puffs, and purchases
       for three or four days.

Unless, of course
       the show's for the birds,
And all that attend
       are lookers and nerds.

But it's my life
       This "Doing the shows."
How I survive it,
       nobody knows.

"Hope springs eternal"
       so optimists say.
I guess I agree,
       I welcome today.

www.ingramcontent.com/pod-product-compliance
Lightning Source LLC
Chambersburg PA
CBHW060551100426
42742CB00013B/2516